DOVER GAME AND PUZZLE ACTIVITY BOOKS

Spooky Mazes

Ted Lavash and Victoria Fremont

DOVER PUBLICATIONS, INC.

Mineola, New York

Bibliographical Note

Spooky Mazes is a new work, first published by Dover Publications, Inc., in 1997.

International Standard Book Number: 0-486-29926-0

Manufactured in the United States of America
Dover Publications, Inc., 31 East 2nd Street, Mineola, N.Y. 11501

NOTE

You will find a special treat in store for you in this collection of spooky brainteasers. At first glance the 40 mazes look simple enough; but you'll soon realize that solutions go beyond simple guesswork as you attempt to navigate a series of bizarre courses. They require you to successfully perform certain tasks—all of which have challenging objectives, devilish restrictions, and roundabout routes that test your skills. You will need to use your brainpower to solve these puzzlers—but hopefully you will not find that to be an entirely unpleasant sensation! Good luck and happy mazing. If you get stuck take a peek at the activities starting on p. 41.

Creepy Place

Be careful of the barbed wire and avoid the creepy eyes when you go through this maze.

start here ↘

end here

In Circles

Can you get out of this maze without going into the monster rooms? You must pick up the key to get out!

start

out

Boo!

Find your way through the maze without disturbing the ghost.

enter

end

Snakes Alive!

Be careful not to touch the poisonous snake on your way out.

in here

out here

The Spider's Web

Can you weave your way through the spider's web without getting caught?

enter here

out

Mummy's in the Way!

Can you get out of this maze without running into the dreaded mummy?

Get All Six

Go through all six rooms in order without retracing your line. Don't go into room X — it's haunted!

start

finish

Skull's Dungeon

Can you escape from the dungeon without passing through any of the skulls?

start here

out here

Yuk Bugs!

Hurry up and get the bug spray to keep the yuk bugs from invading!

start

phew, safe!

BUG SPRAY

Around and Around

Don't get dizzy trying to find your way out.

enter

out

Monster Man

Can you find the path that will let you escape from the monster man?

start with any of these

Hurray, you got by him

Bats in the Belfry

Hurry up! Get out of this maze before you run into a spooky bat.

in here

out

Thunder and Lighting

Work your way through the lightning bolt to get safely to the ground. •

start

to safety

Gruesome Caves

Watch out for the falling rocks as you go through the gruesome caves.

go in here

out

Scary Woods

Get out of the scary woods. Watch out for the spider!

go in here

out

Ants in Your Pants

Run, before the giant ants get in your pants!

in here

out

Graveyard Shift

Can you find your way through this spooky, moonlit graveyard?

enter

out

The Witch is Watching

Hurry out of this maze before the witch casts a spell on you.

in

out

Skeleton's Closet

This secret closet has two doorways. Can you get out without running into the skeleton?

enter

You're ok

The Giant Spider

Find your way out before the deadly spider catches you in his web.

enter

out

Pirate's Gold

Get the gold before the pirate comes back and gets you!

start

you got it!

Crocodile Crossing

Hurry up and cross the bridge that leads you to safety. The crocodile is watching.

enter here

out here

Look Out Below!

Run! Get out of this maze before the monster pulls it down!

start here

you're ok

The Swamp

Cross the bridge that will take you over the swamp and out. Watch out for the quicksand!

enter here

out here

The Pits!

Can you find your way to safety without falling in any of the scary black pits?

in here

out to safety

The Jagged Blades

Cross over the jagged blades and get out without getting cut.

start here

out here

Vampire's Lair

Get out before the vampire gets you!

start here

out here

Get Over the Gorge

Don't fall in the gruesome gorge. Cross the bridge to find your way out.

start

out

Ugly Worms

Start at the top and find the right path through the ugly, icky worms.

start at any opening

safe

This Will Grab You

Beware of the clammy hand! Don't let it grab you.

start

safe

The Secret Skull

You must circle the star over the skull's head before you can get out.

Try this way   or this one   or here

out to safety

Swamp Creature

Don't let the creature pull you into the slimy swamp!

in here

out here

Deadly Daggers

Stay away from the deadly daggers or they will cut you to pieces!

go in here

get out here

Save the Witch's Cat

Go in, circle the cat, and find your way out before the witch comes.

in here

out here

Oh Rats!

The rats are chasing you! Choose the rat hole that leads you to safety.

you can start here

or over here

safe

Sleeping Giant

Shh! Don't wake the sleeping giant as you go through his maze.

in here

ZZZZ

out here

Dark Phantoms

You're being watched by frightening phantoms. Get out as fast as you can.

in here

get out here

EEK! Mice!

These mice aren't nice. Don't waste a minute; get out as fast as you can!

go in here

get out here

The Challenger

Get out your timer. You have five minutes to escape before one of the spiders bites you!

start here

out

Haunted House

Make your way through the haunted house.

Start here

out here

Puzzle Solutions

Creepy Place, page 1

In Circles, page 2

Boo, page 3

Snakes Alive, page 4

Spider's Web, page 5

Mummy, page 6

Get All Six, page 7

Skull's Dungeon, page 8

Yuk Bugs, page 9

Around and Around, page 10

Monster Man, page 11

Bats in the Belfry, page 12

Thunder and Lightning, page 13

Gruesome Caves. page 14

Scary Woods, page 15

Ants in Your Pants, page 16

Graveyard Shift, page 17

Witch is Watching, page 18

Skeleton's Closet, page 19

Giant Spider, page 20

Pirate's Gold, page 21

Crocodile Crossing, page 22

Look Out Below, page 23

Swamp, page 24

Pits, page 25

Jagged Blades, page 26

Vampire's Lair, page 27

Gorge, page 28

Ugly Worms, page 29

This Will Grab You, page 30

Secret Skull, page 31

Swamp Creature, page 32

Deadly Daggers, page 33

Witch's Cat, page 34

Oh Rats, page 35

Sleeping Giant, page 36

Dark Phantoms, page 37

EEK! Mice, page 38

The Challenger, page 39

Haunted House, page 40